The Light Within

Then and Now

by
Rex Ambler

Pendle Hill Pamphlet 425

Pendle Hill pamphlets are not free since the publication of this series continues and does require resources. Please consider making a small donation to Pendle Hill. If you enjoy the whole series you may wish to subscribe to the Pendle Hill pamphlets, ensuring you get the newest releases first.

Requests for permission to quote or to translate should be addressed to:

Pendle Hill Publications
338 Plush Mill Road
Wallingford, PA 19086-6023
Email: publications@pendlehill.org

Publications staff: Shirley Dodson, Janaki Spickard-Keeler
Pamphlet edited by Chel Avery and designed by Mary Helgesen Gabel
Cover photo © 2002 Leif Skoogfors

The Light Within: Then and Now

The Light Within is a fundamental concept of our Quaker faith. We could say that it is the central concept, around which the others revolve. But it is also a remarkably vague concept. Friends use it quite freely to refer to a whole range of ideas and experiences, but there is little sense of a secure and lasting meaning grounded in our history or in our own experience. This ambiguity affects all of us. How do we make sense of our faith, intellectually, without clarity on this central idea? How do we communicate our faith to others? If you were asked by a nonQuaker, for example, to explain what we Quakers mean by it, what would you say?

Consider this definition of the Light from Margery Post Abbott in the recently published *Historical Dictionary of the Friends (Quakers)*:[1]

> LIGHT: The Light is within though from without, and if a person stands in the Light, responds to Christ, and is obedient, the power will be given to the individual to end all his or her wrongdoing…In the 21st century continued unease exists among some (Orthodox) Friends when the term is used without a clear indication that the Light is of Christ as identified with the historic Jesus. Liberal Friends have taken to heart the early Quaker assertion that the Light is available to all people even if they know nothing of Jesus… The Light, often spoken of as the Inner Light, has become a unifying phrase among liberal Friends because of the

multiple ways it can be interpreted, ranging from views similar to those of George Fox to the more frequent sense of the Light as a universal force of love and discernment which is present in the human heart.

It is, I think, a fair account of the variety of Friends' understandings, so long as we include among Friends the more conservative and evangelical wings of the movement in America and elsewhere. But it does not come across as a coherent concept. It is "within though from without." It is "of Christ as identified with the historic Jesus," yet it is a "universal force of love and discernment." Even if we take one of these definitions, we can still ask with some puzzlement, "What exactly does the Light refer to, then?"

What I want to suggest to you is that we cannot answer that question because in the course of our history we have forgotten. We knew once, when our movement started, but life has changed since then, and we can no longer recall what our distinctive language meant, and what it could mean today. So let us begin our inquiry by taking a brief look at what happened.

A brief history

If George Fox's writings were clearer we might have kept that original meaning in mind. This difficulty has been something of a frustration for me personally, since I have seriously wanted to know what George Fox was trying to say, so I have studied those writings in detail with the hope of understanding what he meant by the key concepts that he used. It has been something of a revelation. I will try to explain that meaning in the course of this essay, but I want now simply to indicate how the meaning could have become lost.

The first thing to note is that Fox's message, and that of other early Friends, was new and radical. It was, you might say, a radical answer to radical times. With the king deposed, the church divided, and even the Bible called into question, there was a desperate search to find something or someone that could really be relied on. People looked to new and different theologies and political ideas, but Fox had something new and different altogether. He said, "Your teacher is within you, look not forth,"[2] that is, "Your teacher is inside you, so do not look outside." Do not look to preachers and books, not even to the Bible, but look to the resource you already have inside you. This will teach you what you want to know. Or better, this will *show* you what you need to know, because the reality of it is already there if you have eyes to see and a light to see by. There's the point. As Fox said in two of his simplest statements about the light:

> *The light is that by which ye come to see.*[3]
> *For with the light man sees himself.*[4]

The Light, as he understood it, was not something you saw in the distance, like a beacon or a lamp to entice you on. It was something you saw *by*, like the light of the sun or moon. It enabled you to become aware of the reality around you, and indeed of the reality inside you, but which you could not normally see because of the dark. He was using "dark" and "light" metaphorically, of course. They were in fact regular metaphors of the time for the human condition of knowing or not knowing the truth. The English reformer William Tyndale had said a century before, "All that lie in ignorance are called darkness."[5] And one Francis Rous, writing some twenty years before Fox, but anticipating him, said, "The soul has two eyes—one human reason, the other far exceeding that, a divine and spiritual Light.... By it the soul doth see spiritual things as truly as the corporal eye doth corporal things."[6] Like Fox, he too was echoing the language of the Gospel of John, where light and darkness are described as the opposing realities of human life, so that it is only when humans are healed of their blindness or come out of the dark that they will see "the truth" that will "set them free."[7]

For all that Fox was anticipated by other spiritual writers of his time, and indeed by the Bible itself—when read in the light and with open eyes—Fox's message was new and startling. He was telling people that they had the light of God within them and that, if they could open themselves to it, it would show them all they needed to know. On the questions that most deeply concerned them in life, nothing else was essentially required. The corollary of this brave declaration was that until that inner awakening took place, people were living in the dark. They may have been learned, pious, or experienced in the ways of the world, or of religion, but if they did not really experience the reality they were talking about, they were of no help to themselves or to anyone else. In fact, trusting preachers, books, or religious rites to get you where you really wanted to be was a positive hindrance.

This message was not welcome in the hierarchy of church and society, as you can imagine. It was far too subjective and individualistic. It was disrespectful of learning and authority and, what was worse, it threatened to undermine the given structures of society by persuading people to trust themselves. The result was inevitable. The church and state persecuted the Quakers with the full intention of eliminating the movement altogether. They nearly succeeded. But fortunately (for us) the Quakers held out, trusting the Light Within, which had done so much for them. And they put out a strong defense. The educated among them wrote some impressive books setting out their case, explaining that the Quaker movement was a recovery of the original intention of Christianity, "primitive Christianity revived" (William Penn), and soundly corroborated by the Bible itself, which Christians generally accepted as the basis of their faith.

Robert Barclay's book, *An Apology for the True Christian Divinity* (1676), was the most effective, a brilliant piece of theological argument, which did as much as anything to establish Quakerism as a respectable, law-abiding, Bible-reading religion. But it also had a negative effect. It established the idea that Quakerism was not only compatible with reason and the Bible, which had been Barclay's intention, but also that it was *based upon* them. By defending the Quaker way so successfully by the criteria of the society against which Quakers had protested, he seemed to be accepting those criteria as the most important for himself and for Quakers. Although accepting in theory that the Quakers depended on the Light within them to show them the truth,[8] he interpreted this truth by drawing it from scripture[9] and from the theologians who had interpreted it in the past. The Light was then reduced to a God-given faculty in humans which enabled them to recognize the truth of what these authorities had said, very much as Calvin had said in his pioneering work of the Reformation. The Light was an "organ" that enabled people to see spiritual realities, a secret "vehicle" within them that carried the Divine Presence.[10]

We can also see in retrospect that what Barclay did in trying to defend his persecuted people was to play down those elements of their faith that had provoked the persecution in the first place, that is, their rejection of external authority and their affirmation of their own internal resources. This softening of the critique appealed to Friends too, naturally enough, since by now they were weary of persecution and worried for their future survival. For the next two hundred years or so they accepted Barclay's defense as the very best guide to the meaning and basis of their faith. They continued to affirm the Light Within, and they continued to "wait in the Light" for illumination and guidance, but it had ceased to have the dynamic and transformative role it had had at the beginning. They continued to affirm the truth that the Light revealed to them and to live by it, but it was no longer the truth of their own life, the reality of everyday, which each Friend could see for himself or herself, but a distinctly religious truth about God and his will, somewhat abstracted from their everyday experience. The Light Within now took second place to the Text without.

The lack of clarity in our basic understanding as Quakers is still a problem, therefore. We have been attracted to one philosophical or religious position after another, as we have faced different crises and challenges in our history. But in the process we have lost our distinctive understanding and therefore much of the vibrancy and power of our distinctive faith.

A closer look at the original meaning

The meaning has not been entirely lost, however. In the various changes in our history, some earlier understanding has been revived or renewed, even as something else has been lost. We have enough of a sense of what our faith is about to stay with it and practice it as best we can. We also have enough of a sense of it to recognize it when we meet someone who really lives it, or read a spiritual writing, even of a nonQuaker, which seems to express it well. I have found this myself, in my study of Hindu and Buddhist writing, especially of Gandhi. But I have also found it in the writings of the very first Friends, and this has been doubly exciting for me: not only have they told me more clearly than I knew before what it might mean to be Quaker (and what the Quaker movement might be), but they have shown me the richness and depth of our own tradition, which we could learn to draw upon again.

At the center of their understanding, as I have shown already, was a clear understanding of the Light of God within people—clear at least until Barclay tried to explain it to the intellectual opponents of the Quaker faith. They, the Quakers, knew what it meant to "turn to the Light" and to "walk in the Light." They also knew that as and when they did so, it gave them great clarity in their lives and a deep resolve to live by its truth, even when this was opposed by the society in which they lived. It gave them a sense of unity too, a real Friendship, as they discovered "in the Light" the deeper bonds that held them together. All this they "knew experimentally," even without a clear *intellectual* expression of their truth.

Let me try to articulate what that understanding was—we can consider later how that understanding might be valid for us. I have described it already in broad outline, emphasizing those features which provoked opposition and persuaded Friends eventually to change their view. So let us look in more detail at what it meant for those very first Friends and for George Fox in particular. I think I can describe it under three general statements.

1. The Light was a capacity for awareness in every human being.

We have already heard Fox's brief assertions:

> *The light is that by which ye come to see.*
> *For with the light man sees himself.*

These are, of course, metaphorical uses of the word "light," but drawing obviously on a quite literal meaning of the word: the light of the sun, for example, is what makes the world visible to us, what makes us aware of it. What enables us to "see ourselves," however, is not a physical light but a spiritual one, and the "seeing" is what we might now refer to as insight or awareness. What is more, the source of this light is not external to us, like the sun, but internal, a "light within," like reason or conscience, which at that time were also referred to as "lights within." Yet with Fox and the Quakers, as we shall see, reason and conscience are not adequate to the task of enabling us really to see ourselves. They are too wedded to the ego, which may not *want* to see the reality. So we need a "light of God" to expose the deeper realities in which our lives are involved. We have noted too how those deeper realities can be invisible to us because we have turned a blind eye or have chosen to live in the dark.

The reality of life can be very demanding and even scary, so we do not normally take it all in. We select what we want, and we make up the rest to suit our needs and desires. It is an innocent enough ploy to deal with harsh reality, but it is devastating in its results. It detaches us from reality, and our images and ideas come to stand in for reality—and to get in the way of our seeing it, even when we need to and want to. Fox called this "living in deceit," which is rather close to what we would mean today by "living in denial." And it is "deceit," in Fox's mind, rather than "disobedience" in the conventional Christian sense, that leads to all the suffering and misery we experience in life. "When once you deny the truth then you are given over to believe lies… O, therefore, tremble before the Lord ye hypocrites, and mind the light of God in you, which shows you the deceit of your hearts, and obey that."[11] By the same token, though, the suffering and misery can be overcome if we can see through the deceit and get to the truth. That may not be so easy, of course, if we are really attached to the ideas and images we have come to rely on in life and if our normal thinking capacity is bent on justifying these ideas and bolstering our self-image.

In Fox's time people were wedded to the ideas of theology as an explanation of life, and they were determined to see themselves as "righteous," that is, as justified in the eyes of God. For Fox himself, though, as with others who became Quakers, these stand-ins for reality were no longer adequate. Reality was asserting itself in the form of serious doubts about what they were taught and serious worries about how righteous they really were or could be. They were open to some deeper or more immediate experience of life that would finally disclose the truth of it. This is precisely what happened to Fox as he became aware within himself of an insight that had nothing to do with what others had taught him but everything to do with how he lived life and experienced it himself. Let me give you one dramatic example from his own account in his *Journal*:

> *But oh, then did I see my troubles, trials and temptations more than ever I had done! As the light appeared, all appeared that is out of the light, darkness, death, temptations, the unrighteous, the ungodly; all was manifest and seen in the light… And then the spiritual discerning came into me, by which I did discern my own thoughts, groans and sighs, and what it was that did veil me, and what it was that did open me.[12]*

The Light showed his "darkness," and what it was that "veiled" him, that is, what it was that obscured his vision so that he could not see things properly. It did not give him knowledge of certain general truths about life, as Barclay suggested; it faced him with the particular reality of his own life, directly. It made him aware of what he was doing in himself, with himself, and with other people, and what the dire consequences of this behavior were. "I did discern my own thoughts, groans and sighs," these deep, inarticulate desires and longings that had motivated his behavior but which he had quite failed to understand or control. To see it all now, "in the Light," was his liberation, for he could see now what he really wanted and how he could get it. He could see himself as he really was and others as they really were, without the distortion or "veiling" of his anxious ideas and images. He was in touch with reality and reconciled to it.

This experience gave him the confidence to tell others what he had found. They did not have to rely on what was handed down to them by others, he told them, for they could see the truth for themselves. And they did not have to rely on external mediations like the Bible or the liturgy, for they had the resource they needed within them as a God-given capacity for awareness and insight. As Fox wrote jubilantly in the *Journal*,

> The Lord God opened to me by his invisible power how that every man was enlightened by the light of Christ; and *I saw it shine through all*.[13]

He is using biblical language to describe this insight—in this case the Gospel of John—but he is not basing his claim on the Bible. It is something he can see for himself, as his eyes are "opened" by the God within him.

As people responded to his message and found that indeed they could access this source of insight within them, they were launched on a journey of discovery together to find the truth of life that could make them whole. Like the explorers who were sailing the high seas to discover a new world, these Quakers were searching themselves with an inner light, and a whole new world was being discovered within themselves. "As there is a world without you, so there is a world in the heart,"[14] Fox assured them. And like the new scientists of their day they were building up their knowledge on the basis of experience, having seen the inadequacy of external authority to establish what is true and right. It was indeed an "experimental religion,"[15] comparable to the new, experimental science, and everyone could try it for themselves, testing the validity of their insights against the facts of their experience, both in the silent meditation of "waiting in the light" and in the living out of their insights in everyday life. As Rufus Jones wrote, "Friends ...have endeavoured to build their religious faith upon the inherent authority of truth. They come back for their basis to the test of experience—to the laboratory of life."[16] They do not so much *believe* a set of truths or values, as *trust* a source of insight that can show them the truth, and then live according to that insight.

2. The Light was revealed first as self-awareness.

This should be obvious from what I have said so far about the Light, but it is one of the most neglected themes of Quaker faith, and has been since the days of Barclay.[17] Even the renaissance Quakers at the turn of the last century, who brought so much of the early understanding to life again, failed to see that the Light first worked its magic on people by opening up the truth about themselves. I think the reason for this must have been that they lacked the dark view of humans that saw them as trapped in their own, egocentric ideas. Rufus Jones, Edward Grubb, and the others of this period had such an optimistic view of human nature, like many in the Edwardian era, that they could see no real obstacle to humans' apprehending reality, provided they sat quietly and paid attention to it. A hundred years on, with two world wars behind us and too many examples of oppression and conflict, we are not so likely to be optimistic. We can recognize the huge unconscious drives and motivations that turn people down destructive ways of life, even while they convince themselves they are doing the right thing. So we are more likely to be open to the early Quaker insight that human life is blighted by deceit and make believe, and that therefore the best thing we can do for ourselves and for the world is to find a way of seeing ourselves as we are, free from the anxiety that persuades us to imagine ourselves differently. If we can and do, we will surely then be in a better position to see how the world is and what we may do effectively to improve it.

Fox himself was emphatic that the awareness had to begin with us. "If all men would come to a knowledge of the truth they must come to that which doth reprove them, and lead them into all truth."[18] The implication is that the obstacle to our seeing the truth of life is our idea of ourselves, which tends to leave out those aspects of our lives which we find distasteful or accusing or threatening. We have honed our self-image to make it acceptable to ourselves and others. So what we have to do to get a sense of reality and to become real ourselves is to pay attention to those neglected parts of ourselves and accept them as part of the whole picture. Not easy! There will be much resistance to any such subversive inquiry, and the ego will defend itself vigorously. And how are we expected to become aware of feelings or relationships or actions of ours that we have firmly shoved under the carpet? The early Quakers were very aware of the problem, and they knew it took courage and patience to face the truth about themselves. But they also knew they had the Light as a resource within them that would enable them to see and to accept what they saw. The Light was not involved with the ego or the personality. It would give a detached and holistic view of things, unaffected by fear and prejudice. Its effect then, if followed, was extraordinary. It exposed the pretenses of the ego as biased and self-serving, and so freed a person from egocentricity and "sin." "Which light being owned," said Fox, "self and the righteousness of self come to be denied."[19] And again, in one of my favorite passages from Fox, it is so clear about this inner, liberating process:

Neither lay open one another's weaknesses behind one another's backs… But every one of you in particular with the light of Christ (which he hath enlightened you

withal) see yourselves, that self may be judged out with
the light in everyone. Now, all loving the light here no
self can stand, but it is judged with the light; and here
all are in unity, and here no self-will can arise, no
mastery; but all that is judged out.[20]

The self cannot stand up, you see, because it has been
exposed by the Light ("judged out"). It thought it was
central and important and flawless, but it can be seen in the
Light to be none of these things. It can only flourish as it
finds its center in the source of life itself. Being rooted
there, in the deeper self within, it will find it is bound up
with others in the unity of life. This truth, of course, which
must have alarmed the self-centered ego, is in fact far better
for the ego, if it can accept that its true center lies
elsewhere. So the inner dynamic is quite simple: the Light
frees people from self-imposed restrictions by showing
them the truth and by enabling them to be truly themselves.
Which brings us to our last point.

3. The Light revealed the source of life and unity.

When they let go of the self, and all the ideas and people
and objects they had clung to in support of the self, early
Friends discerned a deeper reality within, which felt like
their real selves. But this deep self had a most unusual
quality. Since it manifested itself initially as a light, making
them more fully aware of themselves, it was giving them a
view of themselves somehow from outside themselves. It
was objective and clear, but also—as they accepted what
was shown them of their failures and weaknesses—it was
accepting and compassionate. Fox could even say in the

Journal that it was "love" that had shown him the truth about himself. "That love let me see myself as I was without him."[21] These qualities of an all-seeing, truthful, and compassionate spirit within him were what Fox understood as the qualities of God. He certainly felt himself being enlightened and empowered by something of God within him, "that of God," as he liked to describe it, suggesting the mystery. And by opening himself up to its truth and accepting it, he was connected with God, the source of his own being.

It is because of this experience, I would say, that Fox and the first Friends did not want to say that the Light was "human." Barclay may have confused matters by saying that the Light was implanted by God in some kind of miraculous intervention, but he was right in thinking that this inner resource was quite different in quality from normal human capacities and that it was in important ways opposed to the typical ego-centeredness of human behavior. This opposition between God and humans was not, I should add, a "metaphysical dualism," as Jones and Grubb called it,[22] suggesting it was built into the nature of things and that it was inherently impossible that humans should be at one with God. It was what we might call a moral or existential dualism, that is, a tragic sense that humans are cut off from the ultimate source of their lives because, out of fear for their egos, they have turned away from it. But when they turned back to that reality, however it was manifested to them, and found their true center in that of God within them, they were freed from the tyranny of the ego and could experience their oneness with God.[23]

By the same token they could experience their oneness with other people. Their old sense of being separate from others, either as individuals or as the group they identified with, was shown in the light to be false and illusory. "Abiding inwardly in the light, it will let you see one another and the unity one with another."[24] Over time, of course, people of influence had constructed great barriers to keep others at bay, barriers of class, religion, and nationality, for example, and they tried to persuade themselves and others that these divisions were inevitable and even beneficial.[25] The early Quakers were not persuaded, however. They saw through the pretense. And much of their lives were devoted to exposing the pretense, pulling down the barriers, and helping people to recognize their essential oneness. This was the point of their various "testimonies": they were trying to act out in their everyday lives the truth about life which they had discovered for themselves, in the hope that the people they encountered would then recognize that truth and accept it.

But they could also see why people acted as they did. Their own experience of being enlightened enabled them to see how other people were caught in the same trap. It gave them a sense of commonality with others even in the dark and difficult experiences of life. Far from feeling superior, their experience gave them a real sympathy for others, and they could see immediately how they might provide help. Having discovered deceit in themselves, for example, they would recognize it more easily in other people. Here is William Penn on the early Quakers with a remarkable insight and a wonderful image:

God, having given them a sight of themselves, they saw the whole world in the same glass of truth, and sensibly discerned the affections and passions of men, and the rise and tendency of things.[26]

So, with the help of the Light, the "glass" or mirror that reflected the truth, they could see through the poses and pretenses in which people liked to present themselves to the feelings and attitudes that really motivated them. In this way Friends got to know the world well, from the inside, as it were, and they knew then how to act in the world so as to make a real difference. But in seeing through others' presentations of themselves, they could also recognize that core of truth and rightness that they had discovered in themselves. As Fox said, "I saw it shine through all." It was a strange double perception. They could see the root of evil in others, in their denial of the truth, but they could also see the root of goodness in others, in their deep (if unacknowledged) awareness of truth. The Light in Friends enabled them to recognize and acknowledge the Light in others, even if the others were unwilling or unable to recognize it. So the Friends discovered their mission in the world: to bear witness in word and deed to the Light in every human being so that they could become aware of it in themselves and live their lives on the basis of it.

Stir abroad whilst the door is open and the light shineth; and so go on in that which letteth you see the world, to comprehend it and to see what is imprisoned by it and suffereth by it. So the Lord give you an understanding in all things.[27]

The Light does all these things and many more things that I have not described by making people aware of who they really are. It is as simple—and as difficult—as that. It shows up all sorts of conflicts and hurts and miseries, but these are seen to arise from a denial of some part of ourselves (or of society), so that seeing those aspects of ourselves we have denied and acknowledging them serves to integrate them into a new kind of unity (both in ourselves and in society).

All they that are in the light are in unity; for the light is but one.[28]

Through the light that enlighteneth them they have life ... they have salvation, they have truth, they have peace with God.[29]

So the Light is known by what it does. And it does many things, beginning with those promptings in our consciences that there is something in our lives that needs attending to. As we attend to it, in silence and stillness, we begin to see the truth of what is going on. And the more we open ourselves to its truth, the more the Light does for us. These various aspects of the Light's activity, and the sense of a process as we move from one aspect to another, were brought out well by another early Friend, Elizabeth Bathurst. In her work *Truth's Vindication*, she set out to defend the Quaker faith by showing how it arose from experience and how it was confirmed by scripture. The opening words of Part II can serve as a summary of that early understanding, using the biblical language that would have been familiar to her as well as her opponents:

21

Concerning the Principle of Truth

What it is, from whence it comes
and whereto it leads.

It is a principle of divine light and life of Christ Jesus,
placed in the conscience, which opens the
understanding, enlightens the eyes of the mind,
discovers sin to the soul, reproves for it and makes it
appear exceeding sinful, quickens such as accept and
believe in it, though they were dead in trespasses and
sins, makes them alive to God, and brings them into
conformity to the image of his son Christ Jesus, that he
may be the first born among many brethren... [cf.
Ephesians 2 and Romans 8].

Christianity does not consist in the belief of so many
doctrines, articles and principles (as some suppose) but
in conformity unto that one eternal principle, to wit,
the light of Christ manifest in the conscience, and yet
leads into a heavenly order both in doctrine, principle
and conversation.[30]

A reflection on its meaning today

That early understanding of the Light was very different
from the understanding we may have as moderns. There is
a difference of language, of course, which is inevitable
after so long a time. There is a difference in thinking too,
since it was all worked out before the rise of modern
science, when people understood their lives primarily in
terms of the Bible. We may notice in particular that early

22

Friends were describing their inner lives and relationships without any knowledge of modern psychology. That makes it difficult for us even to understand. It may even tempt us to dismiss their understanding as primitive and ill-informed. This would be a pity. If we spend time to absorb their language and get a sense of the world they lived in, we can begin to appreciate that what they were saying made a great deal of sense to the people of their time, and that it expressed a vision of life that could still speak to people today.[31] But having done that, we still have to ask ourselves the questions: Does it in fact speak to our condition? Is it still relevant and important?

Let us address these questions a step at a time. We could say, to begin with, that *the original meaning was at least clear*. People at the time knew the phrase "the light within," which they took as a metaphor for a capacity within themselves to see the world and understand it. It was a simple contrast with "the light without," the sun, the moon, or an oil lamp for example, which lit up the world from outside. Most people took the inner light to refer to a capacity for thought or discernment, what they would otherwise call reason or conscience. The Quakers differed, though, in saying that "the true light within" was a capacity to see things as they are, to see reality, and that was beyond their normal capacity to think or discern. Human reason was too biased in favor of the self for authentic discernment. They needed a source outside their normal self. Moreover, they needed a source that challenged their normal self and enabled them to get beyond it. It had to be a light of God.

The people of the time understood the Quakers well enough on this point. What they found very difficult were the implications. It required them to give up their familiar sense of self and trust a source within them that was apparently beyond their control. This was worrying. It was particularly worrying for those in power, since it challenged the hierarchies of church and society on which their power was based. It encouraged people to believe that they did not need to rely on their superiors to tell them how things were or how they were to behave, since they had "something of God" in them that would let them see reality for themselves. The fact that the church and state persecuted the Quakers for their first thirty years or so indicates that in this respect at least they understood Quakers' message very well.

That aspect of their message has some relevance for us, since we moderns are still inclined to look beyond ourselves to find the truth we need to live by, even though we insist we each have the right to decide things for ourselves. We claim to be independent, but in fact we depend a great deal on others. We do not have the rigid hierarchies of the seventeenth century world, but we do have structures of power, less visible perhaps, that determine how we live, and we look to authorities of a different kind, experts or teachers or even celebrities, to tell us what to think. We want to be shown what to believe, what values to take on, rather than to consider for ourselves how reality is and how we should respond to it. Do we need to recover that immediate sense of reality?

That clear understanding of the Light was also the basis of the early Quaker movement, so in that sense it *clarifies our origins* as Quakers. Our movement began, we might say, in this protest against authority in matters of the spirit and in this affirmation of the human spirit to discern what is right. This is not to say that those early protesters had an easy alternative, or that they believed, naively, that everybody could work it out for themselves, without help from others. They knew that they had to dig deep, and they needed one another to support them in this quest. But they had experienced enough of that deep spirit within them to trust it and follow it. They knew they had to wait patiently and to be disciplined in their stillness and silence until the hidden light within them enlightened their lives and the way ahead. And they knew they had to listen to one another as each bore witness, and then to sense what the spirit within them all was telling them about the situation that concerned them. In keeping to this discipline they found that it worked. They came into unity. Their insights were confirmed as they put them into practice. Friends had a sense of being grounded in reality and truly bonded together. This was indeed an "experimental" religion, like the experimental science that was being developed at that time.

If we were to take that approach seriously today, we too would have to be actively involved in experimentation. We would have to sit lightly by our treasured beliefs and values and put them to the test in experience. That would not be easy for us liberal Quakers, since we have generally accepted the idea that all of us have the right to develop our own beliefs, and that we can do this by thinking them through. We tolerate the views of others, but we do not, on this modern understanding, have to agree with them or come into unity. Nor do we have to test our views by an experience that takes us deeper than thought. So here is another challenge for us to consider.

Rather more encouraging perhaps is the realization that, though we may have lost the understanding of the Light that inspired the Quaker movement at the beginning, we have kept the practice. Or at least, we have kept much of the practice. We still sit in silence, we still look for unity in business meeting, we still insist on the nonviolent resolution of conflict. This continuity is remarkable given the changes in our outlook that I described earlier. We obviously value these practices. But why? We are relying on something deep within us to show us the way. But we are almost lost for words to say what this is, or what in fact happens when we trust it. This is where our history can help. It tells us what it means to be enlightened and how the experience can be prepared for and nurtured.

The Light Within makes sense of our practices. We too sit in silence so that our minds can stop chattering and we can begin to hear a voice deep within and feel a Light that will show us what is happening. We look for unity in meeting for business because we are trying to get beyond our individual viewpoints to an understanding we can all share, that is, the truth of the situation we are concerned about. And we refuse to use violence in conflict because we want to reach that deep center in other people which already senses the truth and would secretly like to trust it. In all

26

these ways the light brings people to an awareness of the reality they share so that they can all embrace it and so find real fellowship together.

This understanding opens the way to a new approach for our Quaker life, a much more conscious, deliberate, and committed way of being Quaker. In particular *it points the way to a deeper practice*. It is one thing to sit quietly and ponder the concerns of our life in the hope that some bright idea might occur to us that shows us what to do. It is another thing to let go of our ideas, give up thinking and fantasizing, and wait patiently for the reality of the situation to be disclosed to us. It involves a greater commitment to truth, even when it goes counter to what we want to think about the situation, or makes us feel uncomfortable about ourselves. To give an example: when there is a conflict in our family, or a tension in our meeting, we can respond in a number of different ways. We can quietly ignore it in the hope that it will eventually go away. We can think about it seriously and talk it through with others. Or we can sit quietly and open ourselves up to what is really happening here, not least to the part we ourselves may be playing in this unfolding situation.

My suggestion would be that, if we took our cue from early Friends, we would choose the last option. That might not be the most obvious choice, since we could find ourselves exploring the situation more deeply than we really wanted to, but it might be the most productive. In any case, that is something we can discover for ourselves. Let us experiment more with the options we have. Let us try out the possibilities of this early Quaker practice as we apply it to our own needs and circumstances. Then we shall know what works and what does not. My own experience tells me, as I have tried this over a number of years, that opening myself to the Light in this way makes a huge difference to the way I see my life and the possibilities before me. It gives me a clarity I would not otherwise have and a confidence that the insights I am gaining are grounded in reality and not simply in my own ideas. It convinces me, not that I have found the answer, but that the answer is given when I wait patiently for it.

And finally, does not this understanding of the Light *remind us of our real message to the world?* We know we have something of great value to offer the world, but how do we put it into words? How do we speak to people of our faith without seeming to impose our opinions on them? Our modern understanding of tolerance often takes the form of not challenging other people's beliefs and values, because we fear what their response may be. We fear we might be breaching the line that protects their privacy. Our experience should tell us, though, that most people are hungry for an understanding of life, or a way of living it, that would relieve them of the pain of living as they do. They may be very responsive to a word that tells them of another possibility. If we were true to our Quaker insights we would not be imposing anything on them, since our faith is grounded in an experience of discovery, rather than a set of debatable beliefs. We do not need to argue with people who differ from us. We bear witness to what we know from our own experience and we leave it to others to decide whether and how that witness might be relevant to them. So we can tell them quite confidently, on the basis of our experience, that there is a capacity in us humans to see the reality of life as we each have to live it and that that reality can be trusted, difficult as it might appear, so long as we bring our lives into conformity with it. We can assure them that they do not have to believe the dogmas that are taught them, whether religious or secular, they do not have to put up with the conflicts or oppressions that seem to be inevitable, and, whatever situation they are in, there is always a way to peace and liberty if they follow the Light within them.

If they find our words puzzling or odd, we can give up words altogether and allow our lives to do the talking. "Let your lives speak," we say, echoing early Friends. Our lives can convey our message, maybe even more effectively than words can, because they exemplify what it means in practice to live in the Light of God and follow the truth it reveals to us.

Discussion Questions

1. How would you define the Light? How would you explain the Light to someone who is not a Quaker?

2. The author cites two brief statements from George Fox: "The light is that by which ye come to see," and "For with the light man sees himself." What do these statements mean to you?

3. The author writes, "The Light Within now took second place to the Text without." Why is this a concern, and why does it matter?

4. Why does the author believe that "reason and conscience are not adequate to the task of enabling us really to see ourselves"?

5. The author writes of Quakers: "They do not so much believe a set of truths or values, as trust a source of insight that can show them the truth, and then live according to that insight." Explain.

6. What does it mean to be "judged with the light", and why did early Friends find this experience so powerful?

7. Why is the Light not "human"? How does the Light connect people at a profound level with each other?

Endnotes

1. Edited by Margery Post Abbott, Mary Ellen Chijioke, Pink Dandelion, and John William Oliver Jr., published by The Scarecrow Press, Lanham, Maryland, and Oxford, revised edition 2012.

2. George Fox, a paper of 1652 in *The Journal of George Fox*, ed. John Nickalls, Cambridge University Press, 1952, p. 143; also in the anthology of George Fox by Rex Ambler, *Truth of the Heart*, 2nd Ed., London: Quaker Books, 2007 (hereafter *TOTH*), 1:1.

3. George Fox, Epistle 34 (1653), in *The Works of George Fox*, T.H.S. Wallace, ed., State College, PA: New Foundation, 1990 [1831 reprint] (hereafter *Works*), 7:42; also in *TOTH* 1:68.

4. George Fox, Epistle 149 (1657), *Works* 7:142; also in *TOTH* 1:81.

5. For reference see "darkness" in glossary of Fox's terms, *TOTH* p. 155.

6. For reference see "light" in glossary of Fox's terms, *TOTH* p. 161.

7. See, for example, John 1:1-18; 8:32.

8. E.g., "Therefore the object of faith, and revelation of the knowledge of God to every true Christian, is inward, immediate and objective," *Apology*, Proposition 2:11.

9. E.g., "Though then we do acknowledge the Scriptures to be very heavenly and divine writings...yet we may not call them the principal fountain of all truth and knowledge, nor yet the first adequate rule of faith and manners; because the principal fountain of truth must be the Truth itself, i.e., that whose certainty and authority depends not upon another" (*Apology* 3:2), yet Barclay insists, later in this section, "We do look upon them [the Scriptures] as the only lit outward judge of controversies among Christians, and that whatsoever doctrine is contrary unto their testimony, may therefore justly be rejected as false. And for our parts, we

are very willing that all our doctrines and practices be tried by them" (3:6),

10. *Apology* 5 and 6:15: "A divine spiritual and supernatural light is in all men; … that divine supernatural light or seed is *vehiculum Dei*;… that God and Christ dwelleth in it, and is never separated from it." A good scholarly discussion of this can be found in Leif Eeg-Olofsson and Montagu Evans, *The Conception of the Inner Light in Robert Barclay's Theology*, Lund, Sweden: C.WK. Gleerup, 1954.

11. George Fox, *Journal* (for 1652), ed. John Nickalls, p. 135; also in *TOTH* 1:45. Cf. Romans 1:26. On the suffering this leads to, see Epistle 223 (1662), *Works* 7:238; also in *TOTH* 1:49: "Everyone keep on their watch and guard, against the enemy that led out from God, out of life and truth. For all the sufferings are by and through him that is out of the truth."

12. George Fox, *Journal* (for 1647), ed. John Nickalls, p. 14; also in *TOTH* 1:75.

13. George Fox, The Journal (for 1648), ed. John Nickalls, p. 33, emphasis mine.

14. George Fox, "A Word from the Lord to All the World" (1654), in *Works* 4:38; also in *TOTH* 1:16. In another tract of the time, Fox refers explicitly to the "new world," and he may well have had in mind, as an analogy, the physical new world that was then being discovered in what became known as America. He is writing to the intellectuals of his

time who mocked his "silent waiting." "All you that be in your own wisdom and in your own reason, you tell that silent waiting upon God is famine to you; it is a strange life to you to come to be silent, you must come into a new world" ("An Epistle to All People upon the Earth," 1657, in *Works* 4:132; also in *TOTH* 1:63).

15. William Penn described it as such at the time, in what is still a convincing and penetrating account of the new movement: "Not that thou shouldst believe upon my authority, nothing less; for that's not to act upon knowledge, but trust; but that thou shouldst try and approve what I write: for that is all I ask, as well as all I need for thy conviction, and my own justification. The whole, indeed, being but a spiritual experiment upon the soul, and therefore seeks for no implicit credit, because it is self-evident to them that will uprightly try it'" ["Epistle to the Reader" in *Primitive Christianity Revived*, (1696), reprinted in William Penn, *The Peace of Europe, the Fruits of Solitude and Other Writings*, ed. Edwin Bronner, London: Everyman, 1993, p. 228.] John Wilhelm Rowntree had described the great history of the movement which he had intended to write with Rufus Jones and William Braithwaite as exhibiting "Quakerism as a great experiment in spiritual religion," in the Preface to the first edition of Braithwaite's volume, *The Beginnings of Quakerism*, 1912, p. v. It is quoted in Hugh Doncaster's Foreword to the 2nd edition, 1955, p. v.

16. Rufus Jones, *The Faith and Practice of the Quakers*, London: Methuen, 1927, p. 52.

17. There is a remnant of the original idea in Barclay, in his fine chapter on worship in which, for once, he allows experience to dictate what he says: "There being also an inward quietness and retiredness of mind, the witness of God ariseth in the heart, and the light of Christ shineth, whereby the soul cometh to see its own condition" (Barclay, *Apology*, 11:7). This could have been a starting point for his consideration of "the truth" that "comes to have victory and dominion over their souls" (in the following sentence), but no connection is made. In fact "seeing one's own condition" seems to play no further role in his setting out of the Quaker path to truth and life.

18. George Fox, "Truth's Triumphant in the Eternal Power over the Dark Inventions of Fallen Man" (1661), in *Works* 4:284; also in *TOTH* 1:72. Cf. John 16:7-13.

19. George Fox, a paper of 1657 in the *Journal* (ed. Thomas Ellwood), in *Works* 1:344.

20. George Fox, Epistle 48 (1653), in *Works* 7:61; also in *TOTH* 1:84.

21. George Fox, the *Journal*, ed. John Nickalls, p. 11.

22. Cf. Edward Grubb: "For them [the early Quakers] as for other Christians of the 17th century the world was an *unmixed dualism*. The "natural" and the "spiritual" stood confronting one another but never mingling. God and the world were separated by an unbridged chasm" (*Authority and the Light Within*, p. 80). It is surprising then that he did not rethink this judgment when he quoted William Penn, a

contemporary of Barclay, as saying both that the Light was "in man but not of man" and that it was "natural to man to have a supernatural Light" (FN 2, p. 80).

23. The sense that the Light is beyond our normal human faculties might be part of what is meant by saying that it is "within but from without." But this phrase is misleading. It suggests that the Light is shining *into* us from an outside source. This fits in with an evangelical and protestant idea that there is nothing good in us humans and we need a Christ outside us to help, but it does not fit the distinctly Quaker insight that we humans already have this potential within us: "the light that lighteth every man that cometh into the world" (John 1:9). It is perhaps an understandable reaction against those liberal Friends who talk of the Light as if it were little more than reason or intuition, but it does not add to our understanding. It is also sometimes said that "the *inward* Light" that early Friends spoke of is not "the *inner* Light" of liberal Friends: it is a dynamic movement from outside, rather than a potential within. But this too is a confusion. "Inward" could indicate a direction, as in "inward journey," but it could also indicate location, as in "truth in the inward parts" (Psalm 51:6 in the KJV Bible of 1611), which was its predominant meaning in the seventeenth century. The "inward Light" was therefore simply "the Light inside," as distinct from a physical light outside. (The word "inner" appeared later as an abbreviation of "inward," just as "outer"" replaced "outward" in indicating location. See the full *Oxford English Dictionary* on the history of these words.) But the inward Light was nevertheless different from the light of

reason or conscience, which was merely "human": it was the Light of God, "that of God in everyone," the Light of Christ within.

24. George Fox, in a paper of 1654, in *The Doctrinals: Works of George Fox*, 4:43, also in *TOTH* 2:18.

25. Consider for example George Fox addressing the wealthy people of his time: "O ye earthly-minded men, give over oppressing the poor; exalt not yourselves above your fellow creatures, for ye are all of one mould and blood; you that set your nests on high, join house to house, field to field, till there be no place for the poor, woe is your portion. The earth is the Lord's and the fulness thereof"; in a tract "The Vials of the Wrath of God Poured Forth upon the Man of Sin" 1654 (?), in *The Doctrinals: Works of George Fox*, 4:29; also in *TOTH*, 3:49. For "the earth is the Lord's …" see Psalm 24:1.

26. William Penn, *The Rise and Progress of the People Called Quakers*, first published as a preface to Fox's *Journal* (1694), but later published separately; recently republished in William Penn (ed. Edwin Bronner), *The Peace of Europe, the Fruits of Solitude and Other Writings*, London: Everyman, 1993, p.286.

27. George Fox, Epistle 135 (1657), *Works* 7:132; also in *TOTH* 3:12.

28. George Fox, a paper of 1654, in *Doctrinals, Works* 4:43; also in *TOTH* 2:18.

29. George Fox, "To the Turk" (1660) in *Doctrinals, Works* 4:219; also in *TOTH* 1:121.

30. Elizabeth Bathurst, *Truth's Vindication* (1679), reprinted in her collected works as *Truth Vindicated* (1695), part II, p. 72; republished in part in eds. Mary Garman, Judith Applegate, et al., *Hidden in Plain Sight: Quaker Women's Writings 1650-1700*, Wallingford, PA: Pendle Hill Publications, 1996, p. 381.

31. See Rex Ambler in *Quaker Identity and the Heart of our Faith,* London: Quaker Books, 2008.

About the Author

Rex Ambler taught theology at Birmingham University (England) for over thirty years. He now writes mostly on Quaker faith and practice, and travels to many parts of the world to teach Quaker meditation, or "Experiment with Light," helping those interested to set up "light groups" to practice it. See www.experiment-with-light.org.uk. He wrote of his own experiences of the practice in *Light to Live By: An Exploration in Quaker Spirituality* and more recently of the whole Quaker vision inspired by it in *The Quaker Way: A Rediscovery.*

Some of his other publications include *Truth of the Heart*, an anthology of the writings of George Fox, *The End of Words: Issues in Contemporary Quaker Theology*, and *Global Theology*, which reflects on "Justice, Peace, and the Integrity of Creation," the theme of the 1989 European Ecumenical Assembly, where he represented Britain Yearly

Meeting (then London Yearly Meeting). He has run for Parliament as a Green Party candidate.

Pendle Hill

Located on 23 acres in Wallingford, Pennsylvania, Pendle Hill is a Quaker adult education, retreat, and conference center offering programs open to everyone. Pendle Hill's vision is to create peace with justice in the world by transforming lives. Since Pendle Hill opened in 1930, thousands of people have come from across the United States and throughout the world for Spirit-led learning, retreat, and community. Every year, people from many faiths and backgrounds come to experience Pendle Hill's educational programs in arts and spirituality, community activism and leadership training, and spiritual deepening.

Programs are offered in a variety of formats—including weekend workshops, extended online/on-campus programs, and evening presentations. Information on all Pendle Hill programs is available at www.pendlehill.org. Pendle Hill's mission of spiritual education is also furthered through conference services—hosting events for a variety of religious and educational nonprofit organizations, including many Quaker groups.

The Pendle Hill pamphlets have been an integral part of Pendle Hill's educational vision since 1934. Like early Christian and Quaker tracts, the pamphlets articulate perspectives which grow out of the personal experience, insights, and/or special knowledge of the authors, concerning spiritual life, faith, and witness.

A typical pamphlet has characteristics which make it a good vehicle for experimental thought. It is the right length to be read at a single sitting (about 9000 words). It is concerned with a topic of contemporary importance. Like words spoken in a Quaker meeting for worship, it embodies a concern, a sense of obligation to express caring or to act in response to a harmful situation.

To receive each Pendle Hill pamphlet as it is published, order an annual subscription. Please contact:

Pendle Hill Pamphlet Subscriptions
338 Plush Mill Road
Wallingford, PA 19086-6023
610-566-4507 or 800-742-3150
http://www.pendlehill.org/

Made in the USA
Middletown, DE
03 February 2020